# THE
# STEVENSON
# WIT

# THE
# STEVENSON
# WIT

*compiled and edited by* BILL ADLER

Doubleday & Company, Inc., Garden City, New York, 1966

I am most grateful to Elaine Crane, my able research associate, for her assistance in the preparation of this book.

Library of Congress Catalog Card Number 66–11938
Copyright © 1965, 1966 by Bill Adler
All Rights Reserved. Printed in the United States of America
First Edition

Photographs courtesy of United Press International
and Wide World Photos

# CONTENTS

The wit of Adlai E. Stevenson speaks for itself. It is brilliant, incisive, memorable, thought-provoking, and hilarious.

Stevenson's wit and humor ranks with that of Lincoln and Churchill, and for generations to come, men of all nations will be quoting his words.

*Bill Adler*
*New York City*
*July 1965*

# THE
# PRESIDENTIAL
# CAMPAIGNS

Just prior to the 1952 Democratic National Convention, Stevenson made a trip to California which he claimed as non-political. Addressing a gathering of Democrats, he quipped: "I'm here only in case any of you are residents of Illinois who might be having trouble with your absentee ballots."

Listening to a southern governor sing his praises, Stevenson remarked: "I like that man's objectivity."

*1956 Campaign*

While campaigning in 1956, Stevenson asked some children in his audience "How many children would like to be a candidate for President of the United States?"
They raised their hands. Then Stevenson continued, "And how many candidates for President of the United States would like to be children again?" And he raised his hand.

Stevenson closed a speech he was making in Philadelphia after the 1956 election with these words:
"I think I missed my calling. As a matter of fact, I think I missed it twice."

"I don't wish to deprecate the Vice President's [Nixon's] new personality. But I do wish that we might hear some word from him repudiating the irresponsible, vindictive, and malicious words so often spoken by the imposter who has been using his name all these years."

*1956 Campaign*

Speaking at Yale University during the 1956 campaign:
"I am particularly glad to be here at Woolsey Hall tonight because I always enjoy my visits at colleges. Now, whenever I say this I can see most of my entourage wince—particularly those eggheads who surround me, all of whom are hard-boiled now."

While making a campaign speech in Springfield, Massachusetts, Stevenson and his audience were forced to make a hasty retreat indoors when a sudden rainstorm interrupted his speech.
After everybody was safely inside, Stevenson turned to his audience and quipped:
"I really wanted to save you from drowning next January."

*September 20, 1952*

Speaking in Connecticut, Mr. Stevenson paid tribute to the hatmakers of Danbury and Norwalk for their services to "those of us who suffer from corrosion of the hairline."

*September 19, 1952*

During the peak of the Stevenson presidential boom in 1952, Stevenson said:
"I have been asked more questions than the Quiz Kids and Mr. Anthony put together."

"I have finally figured out what the Republican orators mean by what they call 'moderate progressivism.' All they mean is: 'Don't just do something. Stand there.'"

*Hartford, Connecticut*
*February 25, 1956*

"If I talk over the people's head, Ike must be talking under their feet."

"General Eisenhower employs the three monkeys standard of campaign morality: see no evil—if it's Republican; hear no evil—unless it is Democratic; and speak no evil—unless Senator Taft says it's all right."

*1952 Campaign*

In his concession speech after his defeat in the 1952 election, Adlai Stevenson remarked:
"Someone asked me, as I came down the street, how I felt, and I was reminded of a story that a fellow townsman of ours used to tell—Abraham Lincoln.
"They asked him how he felt once after an unsuccessful

election. He said he felt like the little boy who had stubbed his toe in the dark. He said he was too old to cry but it hurt too much to laugh."

During the 1956 presidential campaign, candidate Stevenson joked:

"I'm beginning to think the reason President Eisenhower decided to run again is that he just couldn't afford to retire to his farm in Gettysburg as long as Ezra Benson is Secretary of Agriculture."

"I don't feel like a gift from Providence, and I really don't believe I am. I feel very much like a corn-fed Illinois lawyer who had gotten into the big time unintentionally."

*Denver, Colorado*
*1952*

"It would be a sad thing if a great soldier [Eisenhower] to whom we owe undying affection and gratitude ended up politically between the two Republican parties like that mule I heard about one time that starved to death standing between two stacks of hay, trying to make up his mind which to eat."

*Denver, Colorado*
*1952*

"I hate thieves. I don't like big government. I like free men, free markets, free ideas, freedom to succeed or to fail. But I know that this is the twentieth century; and most of the Republican leaders don't know that."

*Denver, Colorado*
*1952*

Responding to criticism that the Republicans had leveled at Truman's Democratic administration, Stevenson remarked:

"After listening to the everlasting procession of epithets about our misdeeds, I was even surprised the next morning when the mail was delivered on time."

*July 1952*

Early in the 1956 campaign, Stevenson was asked by a reporter if he considered himself a "middle-of-the-road Democrat."

"I am not one of those who believes that you can characterize a philosophy on public issues by slogans. I have never been sure what progressive conservatism means, or was it

conservative progressivism? I have forgotten. And I am not sure what dynamic moderation or moderate dynamism means. I am not even sure what it means when one says he is a conservative in fiscal affairs and a liberal in human affairs. I assume what it means is that you will strongly recommend the building of a great many schools to accommodate the needs of our children, but not provide the money."

In a speech before the Liberal party in New York:
"I have, of course, read about the Liberal party in the published writings of certain columnists and I am aware that you are dangerous characters. I am fully informed that attacks on you from the right are equaled in violence only by the denunciations which you receive in the Communist press. Well, I know how that is; in my brief political career I've sometimes wondered if I had any friends left. Then they nominated me for President, and now I sometimes wonder if I don't have too many friends!

"I hope that alert members of the press will note that I arrived here under my own power . . . I am standing on my own feet and, to the best of my knowledge, I have been neither drugged nor hypnotized. I offer these testimonials in advance since . . . . I am alleged to be in a state of multiple captivity and you either are or soon will be on my list of distinguished jailers.

"I have been much interested in the continued debate raging in the newspapers as to whether I am headed left, center, or right. I think it would be more relevant to ask: Is the man moving forward or backward or is he grounded?

"We are more tolerant of our quarterbacks than of our presidential candidates. I trust that it will be said of me at least, that I know the difference between the goal line and the sideline."

*New York City*
*August 28, 1952*

"On August 30, three New Jersey labor leaders reported after a conference with the general [Eisenhower] that he did not know the difference between Closed Shop, Open Shop, and Union Shop. When they used the term 'union security,' he said that this was the first time that he had ever heard that term used, but twelve days later, after only a two-hour breakfast with Senator Taft, the general was told, by Senator Taft, of course, that he definitely agrees with the closed shop prohibition and the limited union shop provisions of the Taft-Hartley Law. In two hours the general had become a labor expert. I wonder if Taft's school of labor relations is open to all retired generals."

*1952 Campaign*

As governor of Illinois Stevenson welcomed the Democratic National Convention of 1952 to Chicago with these words:

"In the name of more than eight million people, the people of the State of Illinois, I bring you the heartiest of greetings. As an official of the state, I was very glad to see the Republicans voting their convention in Illinois, but as a Democrat, I am certainly pleased that the amphitheater has a new tenant.

"The previous tenants were very boisterous and noisy and generally obstreperous. The word must have reached them that this hall is often used as a fight arena. They just didn't get along with each other at all. They behaved like people who were out of patience, out of sorts, and out of office. At intervals, they calmed down enough to talk, but then what did they say? Most of the speeches reminded me of that facetious explanation of the word 'auditorium.' It is said that the word 'auditorium' comes from two Latin words, *audio* and *taurus*. *Audio*, of course, means 'I hear' and, as everybody knows, *taurus* means 'bull' . . . As you watched over television, did you notice the quantities of water that the speakers drank? That's the first time I've ever seen windmills run on water power. . . . I have a notion the voters are going to respond in November to those Republican promises the way a certain young lady responded to the proposal of a young farmer friend of hers. He said, 'Marry me and I'll paint the house and the barn inside and out. I'll put in electricity, I'll buy a brand new stove and refrigerator. Will you marry me?' And she said, 'Honey, let's leave it this way, you *do* all those things and then ask me again.'"

On December 13, 1952, a month after he was defeated by Dwight D. Eisenhower in his first race for President, Adlai Stevenson addressed the annual gathering of Washington reporters at the Gridiron Club:

"A funny thing happened to me on the way to the White House!

"The fact was, of course, that the general was so far ahead we never even saw him. I was happy to hear I had even placed second. But no one will say, I trust, that I snatched defeat from the jaws of victory.

"Which reminds me that four years ago, occupying the seat I occupy tonight, was another great governor [Thomas E. Dewey of New York]—excuse me, the governor of another great state—some say the second greatest state in the Union. What just happened to me had just happened to him. In fact, it had just happened to him for the second time.

"But did he dispair? He did not. He said to himself—if I may take a newspaperman's license and tell you what a man says to himself—he said: 'If I cannot be President myself, I can at least make somebody else President.' Which, blast his merry heart, he proceeded to do. Look at him now. He's as contented as the cat that swallowed the canary, or should I say, the cabinet.

"At that Gridiron dinner just four years ago, the newly elected governor of Illinois sat down there with you common people—which reminds me that I rather enjoy talking over your heads—at last! I was happy and carefree and had nothing to worry about; nothing except the organization of a new Administration to clean up the state of Illinois after the long years of the usual Republican misrule.

"I, a Democrat, had just been elected governor by the largest majority ever received in Republican Illinois. And here I am, four years later, just defeated by the largest majority ever received in Democratic America.

"I had not planned it that way. I had wished to continue as governor of Illinois, there to erect a shining temple of administrative purity and political probity. But the gods decreed otherwise—after meeting in the Chicago stockyards. Mindful of the Chinese maiden's philosophical acceptance of unwanted and aggressive attentions, I concluded to accept my fate gallantly and joyfully.

"Now I content myself that it is all for the best. After all, didn't Socrates say that the duty of a man of real principle is to stay out of politics? So you see I'm delighted that the sovereign people have put an even higher value on my principles than I did.

"I am happy that almost twenty-seven million voted for me. I was a little baffled by the emergence of that word 'egghead' to describe some of my supporters. It seems to have been first used to describe the more intelligensiac members of that lunatic fringe who thought I was going to win. I am happy to note you have refrained from saying of the eggheads that the yolk was on them.

"I enjoyed the campaign—in spots. There were times, I confess, when I was afraid I wouldn't die, times when I felt I wouldn't do it to a dog. Let me add, by the way, that, like every red-blooded American patriot, I own a dog. It was not a campaign contribution. And I think the general would say to me that there are times when he wishes he was in my shoes—you see I had them fixed.

"As to my future: Well, there are those like the man who changed the sign on his car after the election from 'Switched to Stevenson' to 'Switched, Bothered, and Bewildered,' who feel that I should devote my classic talents to the welfare of mankind by frequent talking.

"Then there is another smaller group who insist that God and/or the election has appointed me the scourge of the Republican party. And finally there is the much smaller group that feels that it is not wholly unworthy or improper to earn a living. My sons are numbered in the latter group.

"But despite anything that you may have read or written, there are some plans of action that I have definitely rejected. I have declined an invitation to become president of the National Association of Gagwriters. And I will not go into vaudeville. It is equally definite that I will not become manager of the Washington Senators—I mean Clark Griffith's, not Mr. Taft's.

"I have great faith in the people. As to their wisdom, well, Coca-Cola still outsells champagne. They make mistakes. They do sometimes. But given time they correct their mistakes—at two- or four-year intervals.

"I have faith in the people—and in their chosen leaders: men of high purpose, good will, and humble hearts, men quite prepared to stand aside when the time comes and allow even more humble men to take over."

"Whenever the Republicans talk of cutting taxes first and discussing the national security second, they remind me of a very tired rich man who said to his chauffeur: 'Drive off that cliff, James, I want to commit suicide.'"

*1952 Campaign*

"When the Republicans talk about not being able to afford our present defense buildup, I am reminded of the man who refused to put water on his burning house because his water bill was too high already."

*1952 Campaign*

Discussing the Republican platform in 1952 candidate Stevenson made these remarks:

"It is fine as a whodunit, but it isn't very helpful in telling us what kind of domestic or foreign policy the Republicans are going to change to. Standing on it is a little like standing on a bushel of eels, so where is the general to stand? In some fields, he has chosen to jump on to our platform, and in broad daylight. The thing that worries me is that we can't charge him rent. When I practiced law we looked for jokers in a contract. In the Republican farm platform, it is not a question of finding the loopholes in the contract. It is a question of finding a contract in the loopholes."

1952 *Campaign*

Replying to Republican criticism that he used wit in his speeches that was too "highbrow," Stevenson said:

"In a recent speech in Indianapolis, Senator Taft made an attempt at his own brand of campaign humor. He said, laughingly, that he and Senator Jenner and Senator Capehart, the author of the Capehart Amendment, should get together after this speech and decide on campaign policy. If they want to make an issue of campaign humor, let's put that joke at the head of the list. If it is a crime to trust the people's common sense and native intelligence, I gladly plead guilty. I've just been trying to give the customers the right change. That seems to be novel and effete."

*1952 Campaign*

Stevenson's first grandchild was born shortly after the 1956 election. On election night, he ended his prepared concession speech with this comment:

"Let there be no tears for me. If I have lost an election, I have won a grandchild."

*1956*

During the 1952 campaign, there was some disunity in the Republican ranks between the Taft and Eisenhower wings of the party.

After a well-publicized peace conference with Senator Taft, candidate Eisenhower said that party harmony was the first objective of the great crusade.

Mr. Stevenson had this to say:

"I shall not argue that it is necessarily fatal to change horses in midstream. But I doubt if it is wise to jump on the struggling two-headed elephant trying to swim in both directions at the same time."

Upon noting that the platform from which the Republican candidate addressed a Richmond audience had collapsed, Mr. Stevenson commented:

"I'm glad the general wasn't hurt. But I wasn't surprised that it happened. I've been telling him for two months that nobody could stand on that platform."

*Paducah, Kentucky*
*September 1952*

"This whole problem of the need for a change is very interesting to me in a family way. From 1860 to 1912—a period of fifty-two long years—this nation had only one Democrat as President. I can say this with feeling, because, as some of you may remember, Grover Cleveland's Vice President during his second term was my grandfather. I've read a good deal about that period and I don't recall the Republicans during those fifty-two long years saying very much about the sacred principle of change. Evidently 'change' is a sound principle only when the Republicans are out and the Democrats in.

*Illinois State Fair*
*August 14, 1952*

"I had an experience on my last journey to Wyoming that perhaps has been one that many of you have had. Up on top of the Divide, there is that creek that separates and forms the Pacific Creek, flowing down the Western watershed and the Atlantic Creek, flowing down the Eastern watershed. Sitting there on a hot summer afternoon on top of the world, I couldn't help but think of what had happened and what symbolic significance there was in this lovely spot, there on top of the Continental Divide where the winds blow from all directions.

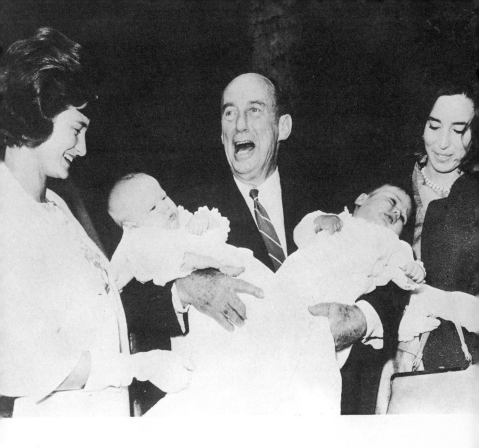

"I thought of how the center of gravity in world affairs had moved in the past three thousand years from the Valley of the Tigris in the Euphrates, the Valley of the Nile to Athens, to Rome, to Paris, to London, and in our time and in our generation had jumped the Pacific and had come to the Western Hemisphere, had come to the United States of America, and somehow, there on top of the Divide, with my feet in the creek . . . I thought of the symbolic significance of the fact that this perhaps was the center of gravity of the whole world, and just at that moment, in my reverie, I dropped my sandwich in the water."

*Cheyenne, Wyoming*
*November 1952*

"My predicament reminds me of the little boy in the radio contest. He was asked to tell, in twenty-five words or less, why he liked this particular program. After considerable effort at finding the most impressive argument he could muster, the boy uttered this testimonial: 'I like the Jack Smith Show because as soon as it's over the Lone Ranger comes on.'"

*Bloomington, Illinois*
*May 1952*

"In the summer of 1933, I served in Washington in the Agricultural Adjustment Administration. I came to this state and spent many weeks conducting hearings mostly at the University in Berkeley for various of your special crops. Among others was a marketing agreement that I wrote for your walnut industry. And here is my sad story: It came Christmas of that year and I received an enormous gunnysack. It stood about six feet high and was full of little Christmas packages of walnuts. It solved our Christmas shopping problem, because we took out the packages and sent them to everybody around Washington. And then I discovered, to my intense chagrin, that in each package was a little card saying 'Merry Christmas from the walnut industry to Adlai Stevenson.' I think that is the last public gift I'll ever receive in public life."

*Modesto, California*
*1952*

"I like fish fries, barbecues, clambakes, and all of the other typical paraphernalia of old-fashioned American politics. . . . That fine old Democratic philospher and picnicker, Thomas Jefferson, saw the point when he said that man had a natural right to 'the pursuit of happiness.'

"I wish that those Republican leaders who like the things

that we have been doing would come over and help us; we welcome them to our picnics.

"I have often told this story—about how I happened to be a Democrat anyway. My mother's family were stanch and longtime Republicans in the State of Illinois and they were members of the Unitarian Church. My father's family were Democrats of many generations, and they were Presbyterians. And by some curious circumstance—I hesitate to call it a deal—when I was born, I ended up as a Unitarian, my mother's church, and as a Democrat, my father's political party. I am a compromise."

*Benson High School*
*Portland, Oregon, 1952*

Stevenson once remarked of Eisenhower's "Crusade":
"The general has dedicated himself so many times, he must feel like the cornerstone of a public building."

Speaking about President Eisenhower:
"Golf is a fine release from the tensions of office, but we are a little tired of holding the bag."

"The Republicans have a 'me too' candidate running a 'yes but' platform, advised by a 'has been' staff."

*Fort Dodge, Iowa*
*1952*

"I have been tempted to make a proposal to our Republican friends: that if they stop telling lies about us, we would stop telling the truth about them."

*Bakersfield, California*
*1952*

"I am, frankly, considerably concerned when I see the extent to which we are developing a one-party press in a two-party country."

*Portland, Oregon*
*May 1952*

"I seem to spend a lot of time reading about myself in papers and magazines these days. The awful thing is, I can't say that I mind it much either."

*Springfield, Illinois*
*July 1952*

"Senator Taft is the greatest living authority on what General Eisenhower thinks."

*Fort Dodge, Iowa*
*October 1952*

"There are two respects in which the Republican leaders have a wonderfully consistent record. They never speak well of Democrats—in fact they don't even speak well of one another any more.

"We have met great needs in the last twenty years; but each move to meet them has been systematically opposed or attacked or undercut by the members of the Party of the Past—the boys whose elephant cannot figure out whether to follow its trunk or its tail.

"Of course, I suppose that all this government activity is what they call socialism—creeping and crawling. I'm no more in favor of socialism than anybody else, and I particularly dislike things which creep. But, if I don't like 'creeping socialism,' there's something else I dislike just as much— and that's galloping reaction."

*Los Angeles, California*
*September 1952*

At a Labor Day rally in the campaign of 1952, a photographer took the famous photo of Adlai E. Stevenson with the hole at the bottom of his shoe. When Stevenson learned that the photographer had received a Pulitzer Prize for the photo, Adlai cabled him:

"Congratulations. I'll bet this is the first time anyone ever won a Pulitzer Prize for a hole in one."

After the 1952 election, Adlai Stevenson received a letter from a man who said his wife sits for hours and cries and "when I ask her what's wrong, she points to your picture and sobs, 'It's him.' "

Stevenson answered: "Tell your wife not to worry—'him's' all right!"

Stevenson insisted he did not want the 1952 Democratic nomination and when a fervent supporter said, "Well, what'll you do if we nominate you anyway?" Stevenson replied:

"Guess I'd have to shoot myself."

At a dinner the night of the Democratic nominating convention in 1952, Adlai Stevenson joked with his sister about the TV camera that had crept up on her from behind that day.

"You'll have to learn how to protect your rear," he said.

From a Stevenson speech during the 1952 campaign on the Taft-Hartley Act:

"I stand before you as a fugitive from a sweatshop down in Springfield, Illinois.

"This is Labor Day of an election year and I think candidates ought to get a day off, too. But if they got off, they might not get in."

*Detroit, Michigan*
*September 1952*

"I had a letter the other day from a man who said that I evidently wanted to put the 'candid' in candidate. Well, I never thought of it just that way before, but I've decided that I could have no better epitaph than 'the man who put "candid" in candidate.' "

*Columbus, Ohio*
*1952*

Speaking in Tucson, Arizona, in the 1952 campaign:

"I am touched and flattered also to find in the audience here this afternoon a lady over eighty years of age who came from my home town in Bloomington, Illinois. You do me great honor, Mrs. Reed, and I should like very much to bundle you into my airplane and take you back to Illinois. In fact we had better take somebody back to Illinois pretty soon, because they are all moving out here."

"Over the door of the National Archives are carved the words: 'All the past is prologue.' And I wonder if that means, in the vernacular, that 'you ain't seen nothing yet'?"

*Albuquerque, New Mexico*
*October 15, 1954*

Speaking at the Senior Class banquet at Princeton University:

"I am informed that this senior class banquet is being held at the expense of your accumulated reserves. I suggest that inviting me here is a very perilous thing to do because certainly within a few hours the Republicans will ask for equivalent time."

*March 22, 1954*

From a speech at Yale during the 1956 campaign:

"Hans Christian Andersen has already written the story of this campaign. He called it 'The Emperor's New Clothes.' All that Estes Kefauver and I have been doing is to tell people what they already know: that the emperor really doesn't have any clothes on at all."

*October 5, 1956*

"You know how it is in an election year. They pick a President and then for four years they pick on him."

*August 28, 1952*

"It would seem that the overwhelming majority of the press is against Democrats. And it is against Democrats, so far as I can see, not after a sober and considered review of the alternatives, but automatically, as dogs are against cats. As soon as a newspaper—I speak of the great majority, not of the enlightened 10 per cent—sees a Democratic candidate it is filled with an unconquerable yen to chase him up an alley."

*Portland, Oregon*
*September 8, 1954*

"I have a special feeling of kinship for Governor Schricker. He's the man who put my name in nomination. But we are still friends. In America any boy may become President and I suppose it's just one of the risks he takes."

*Indianapolis, Indiana*
*September 26, 1952*

"It makes me shudder to think that I graduated from college thirty years ago and how doddering and venerable the thirtieth reunion class looked to me then. If I look to you the way they looked to me, I wouldn't vote for me! Having uttered that sentence, I quickly comfort myself by reminding you that you haven't any younger alternatives."

*University of Wisconsin*
*October 8, 1952*

"The Republicans describe me as a 'captive' candidate. They say I am a 'captive' of the city bosses, and then of the CIO, and then of the Dixiecrats, and then of President Truman, and then of Wall Street, and then of an organization called ADA. Next week that will probably be a girl named Ada."

*Governor's Day Speech at Illinois*
*State Fair*
*August 14, 1952*

"I have been in politics barely four years. There are some politicians who don't think I'm in yet, and others who expect me to be out of it very soon."

*Los Angeles, California*
*September 11, 1952*

"It is not possible for this nation to be at once politically internationalist and economically isolationist. This is just as insane as asking one Siamese twin to high dive while the other plays the piano."

*New Orleans, Louisiana*
*October 10, 1952*

"Brooklyn has meant good fortune for practically everybody except the Dodgers. I will never forget the time I was driving through Brooklyn behind a motorcycle escort; we slowed down at a crowded corner, and I overheard somebody in the curious crowd say, 'It must be dem bums.' I was never more flattered in my life."

*Brooklyn, New York*
*October 31, 1952*

"I am a little like the girl in school who was asked to spell 'banana,' and she said, 'I can spell "banana," but I never know when to stop.'"

*Reading, Pennsylvania*
*October 30, 1952*

"We were driving through the streets of a big city and a little boy ran out in front of the crowd and shouted, 'Hooray for Stevenhower.' I am going to give that kid a job in the State Department."

*Reading, Pennsylvania*
*October 30, 1952*

Shortly after the 1952 presidential boom started for Mr. Stevenson, he was approached by a writer who told the governor he was going to do a biography of him.

"I don't see how you're going to do it," Mr. Stevenson said. "My life has been hopelessly undramatic. I wasn't born in a log cabin. I didn't work my way through school nor did I rise from rags to riches, and there's no use trying to pretend I did. I'm not a Willkie and I don't claim to be a simple, barefoot La Salle Street lawyer. You might be able to write about some of my ancestors. They accomplished quite a lot at one time or another but you can't do anything much about me. At least, I'd hate to have to try it."

"My friends, I have one point to make tonight. That's not many, but it is one more than is made in some political speeches—and that includes some I have delivered myself."

*1956 Campaign*

"There have been remarkable changes in the political scenery since 1952. Four years ago the Republicans rallied the country against the egghead menace. I was pictured then as the leader of the longhairs—despite all surface evidence to the contrary. Things are different today. President Eisenhower no longer ridicules intellectuals, and I note with some amusement that his supporters have organized a committee devoted to the care and feeding of the egghead vote. It even includes college professors. Moreover, a ranking departmental official in the Eisenhower administration has not only read a book but has even written one. And one of the speakers at the Republican Convention was a writer whom Henry Luce periodically loans to the Administration to inject some life—and a little *Time*, too—into the Grand Old Party."

*1956 Campaign*

# FAVORITE
# STEVENSON
# STORIES

One of Adlai Stevenson's favorite religious stories was about a little girl who was busy with her crayons. Her mother asked her whose picture she was drawing. "God," the little girl replied. "But, my dear, nobody knows how He looks," the mother admonished. "They will when I'm finished," the child answered.

Stevenson opened a campaign speech in Seattle, Washington, with these remarks:

"If you treat me this well, you may never get rid of me—so, look out. I have read a lot of stories about the time when my grandfather campaigned in the State of Washington for the Vice Presidency, exactly sixty years ago this month. The big issue, I am told, at that time was whether your majestic mountain was to be named Mount Tacoma or Mount Rainier. Apparently, that was the only subject of interest in Washington at that time. Anyway, the views of Seattle and Tacoma were in violent disagreement and it seems that my adroit grandfather solved this difficulty by giving each audience from the rear platform of his train an eloquent speech about the beauties of the mountain, and then went on to say, 'And I want everyone to know, all of you good people, that I emphatically agree that this mountain should be named—' And just then they pulled the whistle on the train and it started with a huff and a puff, and the old man bowed to the audience graciously and they cheered ecstatically."

*September 8, 1952*

Stevenson told this story to illustrate the alleged difference between Republican acts and words.

It was about a young man whose father had been hanged and who felt humiliation whenever the matter came up. Finally the young man solved the problem with the following explanation:

"My late and lamented parent died in consequence of injuries suffered when the floor of a platform gave way at a public ceremony in which he was taking a prominent part."

After his defeat in the 1956 presidential election, Mr. Stevenson made a speech before the Gridiron Club in Washington.

To illustrate how he felt in losing the Presidency while his fellow Democrats swept control of Congress, Mr. Stevenson told the story of the Lone Ranger riding the western plains with his ever-faithful Indian sidekick Tonto:

"Suddenly, they were encircled by hostile redmen—a thousand Sioux to the front, three thousand Iroquois to the rear, and two thousand Apaches on either side. The Lone Ranger turned to Tonto and said, 'It looks bad for us, old pal.' To which Tonto replied, 'What do you mean, "us," white man?'"

A favorite Stevenson story that he told often:

"I remember hearing a story from a schoolteacher in Chicago one time about a little Jewish boy who came up to her one day and said he would like to be excused from school because it was Yom Kippur and his grandmother wanted him to be at home on that religious holiday. And the teacher excused him. On hearing that, a little Irish boy came up and asked to be excused likewise. The teacher said, 'But, Patrick McCarthy, I know you are not Jewish.' He said, 'No, but I think grandmother is a little Jewish and I am sure she wants me to be at home with her.' Then, by golly, if a little colored boy didn't come up and ask if he couldn't be excused, too. She said to him, 'Well, now, Joseph, this is going too far. I know that you're not Jewish.' And he said, 'No, ma'am, I'm not, but I sure am in favor of this cause.'"

"I feel like the young man who was engaged to marry one of twin girls who had a local reputation for beauty. His uncle asked him one day: 'Well, Dick, my boy, my congratulations. I hear you are engaged to marry one of the beautiful Smith twins. But tell me how on earth do you tell them apart?' To that the young man gave his uncle a broad grin and the glib reply: 'That's easy—I don't even try.'"

*1952 Campaign*

"I feel a little like the old Confederate soldier, unarmed, ragged, and asleep, whom some zealous young Union soldiers captured. 'Get up, Reb, we got you,' they shouted. 'Yeh,' the weary old fellow mumbled, 'and it's a heck of a git you got.'"

*1952 Campaign*

"It is like little Willie's new baby brother. As soon as the baby was born Willie hurried to spread the news around the neighborhood. He was telling his young friend Johnny: 'We have a new baby at our house and it cost a hundred dollars.' To which Johnny replied: 'Gee, a hundred dollars is a lot of money just for a baby.' 'Yes,' Willie agreed, 'but think how long they last.'"

*1952 Campaign*

"When the U.S.O. comes in your community and says 'organize,' don't take the attitude that the lady did when she went to a department store, bought a lot of merchandise, and said, 'Charge it,' and then said, 'Thank God, that's paid!'"

*1952*

"I couldn't help but think of the familiar tale of the three Boy Scouts who were called upon to report their respective good deeds of the day. The first said to the scoutmaster: 'This afternoon I saw an old lady at the corner of Fourth and Main Street and I helped her across the street.' The second boy stepped up hard upon the heels of the scoutmaster's word of approbation and made his report. It was: 'My good deed for the day was to help an old lady across the street at Fourth and Main.' When the third boy came up with the same story, the scoutmaster could not forbear voicing his surprise at the strikingly uniform nature of the services rendered. Whereupon one of the lads, conscious of a Scout's pledge to serve always the cause of truth, spoke up in this wise: 'Well, of course it was the same old lady. She didn't want to cross the street and it took three of us to do the job.'"

*Springfield, Illinois*
*1952 Campaign*

"Perhaps you have heard about the Chamber of Commerce that sent off two letters to a senator in the same mail. One of the letters demanded an immediate and drastic reduction in the federal budget. The other demanded a ten-million-dollar appropriation for a harbor improvement which the Chamber wanted for its home town. You know how it is; anything that helps the other fellow is extravagance; anything that helps you is a necessity."

*Indianapolis, Indiana*
*February 1952*

"It sort of reminded me about the story of the little boy who heard his political father talking about converts and traitors—and he said to him, 'Father, what is the difference between a convert and a traitor?' The father said, 'Well, son, don't you understand, if a Republican becomes a Democrat, he is a convert; but if a Democrat becomes a Republican, he is a traitor.'"

"There is a lesson for all of us in this rallying of our forces from every corner of Illinois. Perhaps I can best illustrate it with the story of the young man who approached the father of his intended bride to seek his approval of the marriage. The father was skeptical. 'I doubt very much,' he said, 'that you

would be able to support my daughter—I can hardly do it myself.' To which the young suitor offered the bright suggestion:
'We'll just have to pool our resources.'"

*Bloomington, Illinois*
*May 1952*

Called upon to speak at a festival when he was governor of
Illinois, Mr. Stevenson joked:

"Perhaps my function [at the festival] is not unlike that
which a rural county judge was once called upon to play. Lin-
gering in his chambers one Saturday afternoon after the close
of the business week, he was suddenly confronted by a young
G.I. who had unexpectedly received a forty-eight-hour leave
and who, having his intended in tow, thought to improve the
time by getting married. The high hopes of the pair were
dashed by the judge's kind but firm explanation that, without

the license which could not be procured because the appropriate offices were closed, the ceremony itself could not be performed. The resulting gloomy silence was broken after a moment or so by the boy's hopeful question—'But, judge, couldn't you just say a few words to tide us over the weekend?'"

While he was governor of Illinois, Adlai Stevenson had a Dalmatian named Artie. On one occasion the governor had this to say about his dog:

"Dogs take on man's best ways. Artie's loyalty is unquestioned but when the master is away Artie becomes lonely and takes to running around the neighborhood covering the same total area he was accustomed to exploring on the farm. Artie's disregard of the city ordinance that forbids such vagabonding brings phone calls from neighbors. You see, most everyone knows Artie. He gets around a lot more than I do. In fact, when I go walking with him it's amazing how many greet us with, 'Hello, Artie.'

"However, he is a source of embarrassment to the police and me. After all, a governor's dog may not have to be above suspicion but he should at least try to obey the law. His confined life here is not according to his nature, so we all try to make allowances."

*Executive Mansion*
*Springfield, Illinois*

"I think of a story my grandfather Stevenson, a devout Scottish Presbyterian, told about the preacher who was driving along a back road in the South when he espied a parishioner wearily clearing up a poor, stony field.

'That's a fine job you and the Lord have done clearing up that rocky field,' he shouted. 'Thank you, parson,' the man replied, 'but I wish you could have seen it when the Lord had it all to himself.'"

*Washington, D.C.*
*January 1959*

Speaking at the Harvard Business School at the National Business Conference:

". . . And the businessman, although he has lost much of his former influence, is still 'central' in and indispensable to the American and world systems. So it is imperative that he, of all people, 'think greatly,' that he assume a more objective and influential role in the larger concerns of the new equali-

tarian society that is emerging here and everywhere in this age of revolution.

"I think of the prayer of a little English boy in World War II: 'God bless Mother and Daddy, my brother and sister, and save the King! And, oh God, do take care of Yourself, because if anything happens to You we're all sunk!' Please don't think that I am equating business and God. I'm a Democrat and you have not fooled me! But the pivotal position of business and the business manager in our society must be obvious to any serious student of our system."

*June 1959*

Addressing the National School Boards Association in San Francisco, California:

"I was flattered by your invitation to make the keynote speech at this convention—in part because I thought I was through with keynotes and conventions. But for me who knows so little about education to talk to you who know so much makes me very uneasy. And at the moment I feel as unsupported and insecure as Hilaire Belloc's water beetle:

> 'Who travelled on the water's face
> With ease, celerity and grace;
> But if he stopped to try and think
> Of how he did it, he would sink!' "

*January* 1959

On the subject of education, Stevenson was fond of quoting a prisoner who once told his cellmate:

"I'm going to study and improve myself, and when you're still a common thief, I'll be an embezzler."

Adlai Stevenson enjoyed telling about the little Irish boy's prayer from Chicago:

"Our Father, Who art in heaven, O'Halloran be Thy name."

Mr. Stevenson had many favorite stories and one was Sholom Aleichem's tale of the Jewish elder who amused his fellow ghetto sufferers. One day the elder told how he and his family were chased across an icy lake by wolves. The ice gave way and everybody sank into the water.

"And what do you think God did for us in that situation?" the elder would ask. "Thanks to Him, the whole story is a lie from beginning to end."

"I remember the story of a man in my home town of Bloomington who was interviewed by a newspaper reporter on his one hundredth anniversary.

"After congratulating the old gentleman, the reporter asked a few questions. 'To what do you attribute your longevity?'

"The centenarian thought for a moment and holding up his hand and ticking off the items on his fingers, began: 'I never smoked, I never drank liquor, and I never overate; and I always rise at six in the morning.'

"To that the reporter remarked: 'I had an uncle who acted the same way but he only lived to be eighty. How do you account for that?'

"'He didn't keep it up long enough,' came the reply."

"I always think of the story about the minister who opened a church conference with a prayer which went something like this:

"'Oh Lord, be with the first speaker and give him power to inspire this group. And be with the second speaker and imbue him with Thy spirit. And Lord, have mercy on the last speaker.'"

On one occasion, Stevenson had to substitute for Vice President Alben Barkley at a Democratic rally in Indiana. Stevenson was a little hesitant about taking the place of Barkley, who was a well-known orator.

"I felt like the motorist who ran over a hog on the highway. The farmer was very irate, but the motorist finally calmed him down and said, 'Don't worry, I'll replace your pig.' 'Replace him!' the farmer shouted, 'you can't. You ain't big enough.'"

"I'm like the little boy who asked his mother if we all came from dust.

"'Yes, that's right,' she replied.

"'Well,' said the boy, 'I've just looked under the bed and there's somebody there, but I can't tell whether he's coming or going.'"

Speaking before a Rotary Club in Nashville, Tennessee:
"It reminds me of a story about a gentleman who addressed a large dinner party much, much too long. When he finally finished, the toastmaster arose and said, 'Samson slew a thousand in a night with the jawbone of an ass. Our guest speaker has just put *two* thousand to sleep with the same implement and in only half the time!'"

*Spring* 1952

While he was governor of Illinois, Stevenson received a letter from a congressman who complained that stationery bearing the watermark of the Illinois state seal was being used by a gambler in letters offering tips on horseracing. This was Stevenson's reply to the congressman:

"Your taste for unverified accusations reminds me of the lawyer who said to the jury: 'These are the conclusions on which I base my facts.'"

Some people say that I have been going to the left; other people say that I have been going to the right. It sort of reminded me of a story I heard long ago about the church that was trying to get a new minister and they said—the committee said—"Now we want someone who is not too conservative, and not too radical. You know, we want somebody just mediocre."

*Albuquerque, New Mexico*
*September 12, 1952*

# THE ART
# OF
# POLITICS

As governor of Illinois Stevenson vetoed a bill which had passed both houses of the Illinois General Assembly. This bill would have imposed fines on owners of cats if they permitted them to run unleashed at large.

After saying he was vetoing the bill for several reasons, Governor Stevenson wrote:

"Furthermore I cannot agree that it should be declared public policy in Illinois that a cat visiting a neighbor's yard or crossing the highway is a public nuisance. It is the nature of cats to do a certain amount of unescorted roaming . . .

"I am afraid this bill could only create discord, recrimination, and enmity.

"Also consider the owners' dilemma: To escort a cat abroad on a leash is against the nature of the cat, and to permit it to venture forth for exercise unattended into the night of new dangers is against the nature of the owner . . ."

Touching on the act that cats try to catch birds, the Stevenson veto ripped the measure apart with sarcasm dripping with acid:

"The problem of cat versus bird is as old as time. If we attempt to resolve it by legislature, who knows but what we may be called upon to take sides as well in the age-old problem of dog versus cat, bird versus bird, even bird versus worm.

"In my opinion, the State of Illinois and its local governing bodies already have enough to do without trying to control feline delinquency.

"For these reasons, and not because I love birds the less or cats the more, I veto and withhold my approval from Senate Bill No. 93."

Stevenson's rule for speechwriting:

> "If you would make a speech or write one
> Or get an artist to indite one.
> Think not because 'tis understood
> By men of sense, 'tis therefore good,
> Make it so clear and simply planned
> No blockhead can misunderstand."

*October 1960*

After his defeat in 1952, Adlai Stevenson made these comments about his presidential campaign:

"Thousands even wrote gracious, flattering letters, after the election, explaining why they did *not* vote for me. They seemed to feel they owed me an explanation. I was touched and flattered, but I confess the thought occurred to me now and then that a little 'X' in the right place on the ballot would have been so much easier than a long, thoughtful letter.

"At least for an inexperienced candidate, I suppose we have contrived few more exacting ordeals than a presidential campaign. You must emerge, bright and bubbling with wisdom and well-being, every morning at eight o'clock, just in time for a charming and profound breakfast talk, shake hands with hundreds, often literally thousands, of people, make several inspiring, newsworthy speeches during the day, confer with political leaders along the way and with your staff all the time, write at every chance, think if possible, read mail and newspapers, talk on the telephone, talk to everybody, dictate, receive delegations, eat, with decorum—and discretion!—and ride through city after city on the back of an open car, smiling until your mouth is dehydrated by the wind, waving until the blood runs out of your arm, and then bounce gaily, confidently, masterfully into great howling halls, shaved and all made up for television with the right color shirt and tie—I always forgot—and a manuscript so defaced with chicken tracks and last-minute jottings that you couldn't follow it, even if the spotlights weren't blinding and even if the still photographers didn't shoot you in the eye every time you looked at them. (I've often wondered what happened to all those pictures!) Then all you have to do is make a great, imperishable speech, get out through the pressing crowds with a few score autographs, your clothes intact, your hands bruised, and back to the hotel—in time to see a few important people.

"But the real work has just commenced—two or three, sometimes four hours of frenzied writing and editing of the next day's immortal mouthings so you can get something to the stenographers, so they can get something to the mimeograph machines, so they can get something to the reporters, so they can get something to their papers by deadline time. (And I quickly concluded that all deadlines were yesterday!) Finally sleep, sweet sleep, steals you away, unless you worry—which I do.

"The next day is the same.

"But I gained weight on it. And it's as tenacious as a campaign deficit!

"And, too, there is mirth mingled with the misery all along the way. They shout, 'Good old Ad-lie!' If you run for office and have a slightly unusual name, let me advise you either to change it before you start, or be prepared to take other people's word for it.. And I shall not soon forget about the woman in the crowd in San Francisco who reached into the car to shake hands with me, and not long after discovered that she had lost her diamond ring. Nor will I forget the warm welcome I received on a whistle stop in Bethlehem and my thanks to 'the people of Allentown.' My only hope is that *they* forget it! Again, out West, I warmly endorsed the impressive chairman of a meeting as a candidate for Congress, only to discover that he was not running for Congress or anything else."

" 'What kind of Democrat I am' makes me feel a little like the old lady who said she didn't know what she thought until she heard what she said. I'm not sure what kind of Democrat I am, but I am sure what kind of a Democrat I am not. I'm not one of those who believes we should have a democratic regime because it is good for the Democratic party. If the Democratic party is not good for the nation, it is not good for me or for Democrats."

Refusing to say in 1960 whether he would accept a draft for the Democratic presidential nomination, if one should materialize, Stevenson told reporters:

"If I told you I would accept a draft, it would appear I was courting a draft. And if I said I would refuse, I would appear to be a draft evader."

"Mr. Nixon is a man who believes that the only thing that counts in politics is whether you win or lose."

*1960 Campaign*

"Mr. Nixon's farm policy is vague but he is going a long way toward solving the corn surplus by his speeches. If he continues, there may be a serious shortage by November seventh. The corn–hog ratio could reach a serious imbalance."

*1960 Campaign*

Explaining to a British audience in July 1959 why he wanted to avoid running for the Presidency again, Mr. Stevenson joked:

"A presidential candidate has to shave twice a day—and I don't like that."

Introducing President Johnson at a Washington dinner:

"Mr. President, you are doing so well that even the Republicans like you. They can find only two things wrong—your foreign policy and your domestic policy."

*March 1964*

Commenting on the 1964 election campaign between President Johnson and Senator Goldwater:

"May the best man win. Unfortunately, that didn't happen in my case."

*St. Louis, Missouri*
*October 1964*

Adlai Stevenson visited Atlanta, Georgia, in November 1953, a year after his defeat in his first campaign for the Presidency.

Remarking on Georgia's delightful weather for November, Mr. Stevenson said he wished he had brought his golf clubs with him and then he quipped:

"Don't construe that as an announcement that I plan to run in 1956."

Speaking to the Georgia delegation at the 1960 Democratic National Convention:

"I came by to thank you for voting for me twice. There are not too many states I can say that about."

Governor Sanders of Georgia turned to Mr. Stevenson and said, "If you decide to run for President again, for the third time, Georgia will vote for you."

"Governor, that's the safest political promise you ever made," replied Stevenson.

As governor of Illinois, Mr. Stevenson once vetoed a pension bill for elderly persons on the grounds that the bill didn't provide for the money to pay the pension.

"I can only assume that the authors of this transparently political gesture were more concerned with raising the hopes of our aged dependents than their incomes."

"Mr. Nixon's defenders insist that although there are certain things in his record which aren't very pretty, he has, nevertheless, shown the capacity for growth and if elected will develop the character for the job. I think it unlikely, however, that the American people will want to send Mr. Nixon to the White House just on the chance that it might do him a world of good."

*1960 Campaign*

Stevenson made this comment about the split in the Republican party between Rockefeller, Nixon, and Goldwater just prior to the 1960 Republican National Convention:

"Originally, the Republicans made their headquarters in Denver until they discovered it was so close to the Great Divide. The unhappy symbol of this phenomenon of nature made them so uncomfortable, they folded their tents and came East. Governor Rockefeller says America is going too slow; Senator Goldwater says we are going too fast; Vice President Nixon says we shouldn't talk about it."

"I hear it said that diplomacy is soft work. But don't you believe it, and if you're desperately in need of a bad attack of ulcers or galloping frustration, just go into diplomacy for a while, and you'll get both."

*Springfield, Illinois*
*February 1948*

"I have read the speech made by our governor [Dwight Green] when he opened the Republican campaign. His speech damns me with being on leave from 'the striped pants brigade to the Roosevelt-Truman State Department.' Damned or striped, I will keep my pants on."

*Peoria, Illinois*
*March 1948*

Speaking at his alma mater, Princeton, in 1954, at a Senior Class banquet:

"In doing my homework this morning on this evening's oration, I glanced at the Nassau Herald of 1922 in the hope that I would find something about myself that would impress you.

"Well, I must say in the long corridor of retrospect, I don't look as important as I thought I was.

"I discovered that when my senior class voted to bestow the sobriquet of 'biggest politician' upon one of its members, I received only eight votes. But when it voted on 'thinks he is the biggest politician,' I won second place, and that was due to a conspiracy among my roommates.

"For the title of 'most likely to succeed' I received the impressive total of two votes."

"Some day I want to come to Hamilton County, Illinois, just to visit. . . . I want particularly to go to Persimmon Ridge . . . and meet its mayor. He has a job, I understand, that would interest me after six weeks of campaigning. I believe his principal responsibility is to see that one street light goes off and on at the right time."

*1948*

"That reminds me of the man who said he hoped we would soon get back to normal. I asked him for his definition. 'That's a condition,' he said, 'where you have 1951 income, 1932 costs, and 1911 taxes, all at one time.'"

*University of Illinois*
*Chicago, June 1951*

After his defeat in the 1952 election, Stevenson made a worldwide tour to take a look at American aid programs. He commented on his trip at a lecture at Harvard University.

"How are we getting along with this appalling undertaking? Out of a job—thanks to the voters—I went to see for myself. Starting from San Francisco in March 1953, with four companions I traveled for six months around the edges of the Communist empire through Asia, the Middle East, and Western Europe. I talked to the Emperor of Japan, the Queen of England, the Pope, and to all the kings, presidents, and prime ministers along my route. And I also talked to countless diplomats, politicians, journalists, students, soldiers, peasants, porters, and multitudes of new and warm-hearted friends. Everywhere I encountered an eagerness to talk and a candor of expression among officials that touched and astonished me—and has heavily taxed my discretion. And often the hospitality made me wonder if my hosts were confused and thought I had been elected President in 1952!"

*March 1954*

Accepting an honorary degree at McGill University:
"I think Bernard Shaw once said that he never resisted temptation because he had found that the things that were bad for him did not tempt him. I wish I could say the

same. But I can't. I find honorary degrees always tempting, and often bad for me: tempting because we all—even ex-politicians—hope to be mistaken for scholars, and bad because if you then make a speech the mistake is quickly exposed.

"This is my predicament here today. I am honored, and you have to listen to a speech. It hardly seems fair."

*Montreal, Canada*
*May 1959*

Mr. Stevenson once characterized the foreign policy of President Eisenhower and Secretary of State John Foster Dulles as:
"The power of positive brinking."

"Nixon is the kind of politician who would cut down a redwood tree, then mount the stump for a speech on conservation."

"An independent is the guy who wants to take the politics out of politics."

Mr. Stevenson once described Barry Goldwater, the 1964 Republican presidential nominee, as:
"A man who thinks everything will be better in the rear future."

"I like Republicans, have grown up with them, worked with them, and would trust them with anything in the world—except public office."

Speaking of the Republican party, Mr. Stevenson quipped:
"The elephant has a thick skin, a head full of ivory, and as everyone who has seen a circus parade knows, proceeds best by grasping the tail of his predecessor."

"There are constant complaints from men who say we are playing a sucker's game of global Santa Claus. Parenthetically, and speaking as a politician, I have never been able to understand this attack on Santa Claus. The attackers imply that he is softheaded and subversive, that there is nothing worse than playing Santa Claus. But surely this can't be good politics. Most of us remember Santa as a good fellow and a very welcome visitor. As a Democrat, I want to speak up for him."

*September 28, 1955*
*University of Texas*

From an address at a Democratic National Committee dinner:
"I don't know why we complain so much about their broken campaign promises. It's those they keep that hurt."

*November 19, 1955*

"Thinking of political influences brings back one unhappy incident of those days. It was a Sunday dinner at grandfather Stevenson's with William Jennings Bryan. From prior visits, I recalled with awe how much fried chicken he could eat and I resolved to match him, piece for piece. I did, and when we reached the great Chautauqua tent for his speech, I promptly fell sound asleep at his feet, to the great discomfiture of my parents. But I still love fried chicken—and Democrats."

In a speech before the 1960 Democratic National Convention:

"I think I know who we are going to nominate at this convention. We are going to nominate the last survivor."

*San Francisco, California*
*July 1960*

In 1960, Stevenson suggested this campaign slogan for Richard Nixon:

"Don't change administrations in these perilous times into which we have led you."

# AMBASSADOR
# TO THE
# UNITED NATIONS

In an address to the American Society of Newspaper Editors in Washington, Stevenson apologized for arriving late. It seems he had been held up at the airport by the simultaneous arrival of President Charles de Gaulle of France. Stevenson shook his head and remarked to the gathered editors:

"It seems my fate to be always getting in the way of national heroes."

Adlai E. Stevenson appeared at a rally for President Johnson with a cast on the middle finger of his right hand.

"I tried to break up a dog fight and I broke my finger, which just indicates the perils of peacekeeping. Perhaps I should have picked them up by the ears."

*October 12, 1964*

When Adlai Stevenson first arrived at the United Nations in 1961 to take his position as United States Ambassador to the UN, he was taken on a tour through the UN Security Council Chamber.

He spotted the United States nameplate at the horseshoe table and was told that he was next in the rotation for the Security Council Presidency.

"That's the way it is," he commented. "When I want the Presidency, I can't have it; when I don't, I can."

"I have been picketed, applauded, and abused from Right and Left and Center everywhere from Texas to Toronto for more years than I like to remember. Indeed, my honorary degree should have DP—a Doctor of Pickets."

*Harvard University*
*June 1965*

In replying to critics of the UN, Ambassador Stevenson cited Adam's proposal of marriage to Eve in the Garden of Eden.

"She hesitated for a moment, whereupon Adam asked, 'Is there somebody else?'"

As United States Ambassador to the UN in New York, Mr. Stevenson was very much in demand as an escort for prominent women.

"Over Christmas," he remarked on one occasion, "I read a story about my glamorous social life. I was squiring Mrs. Kennedy, Ava Gardner, Lauren Bacall, and some gorgeous dame I've never even met."

In a speech in which he emphasized the importance of standing up for the United Nations, Mr. Stevenson remarked:

"Some of you remember the story of the man who had

been consuming alcoholic beverages at a considerable rate, and who went to a revival meeting and fell asleep in the front row.

"The preacher reached a climax of eloquence and called for those on the side of the Lord to stand up. After they all sat down, the preacher hollered: 'Now, anybody on the side of the Devil, stand up.'

"The shout awoke the befuddled man, who stood up slowly, looked around him, and said, 'Preacher, I'll stick by you, but we seem to be in a hopeless minority.'"

After three months of weary crisis debate at the United Nations in May 1961, Mr. Stevenson remarked:

"What with Cuba, Congo, Korea, and now Laos, I sometimes yearn for the simple brutalities of bi-partisan politics."

"You know the story about the man in the restaurant who complained to the waiter that his broiled lobster had only one claw, and the waiter said it lost the other one in a fight; so the man said, 'All right, then bring me the winner.'

"Well, the United States is still the winner in the United Nations."

*June 8, 1962*

A Philippine delegate to an organizing meeting of the United Nations in 1945 asserted that the best way to keep the United States in the United Nations is to put the UN's feet in the United States.

"The danger of American isolation," the Philippine delegate said, "is as great today as ever. And," he asserted, "the United States behaved like an elderly, excited lady about to become a grandmother at San Francisco when she observed the birth pangs of the United Nations organization."

To this delegate Adlai Stevenson replied that he was "shocked to hear his country referred to as an excited grandmother." He went on to say that he had always considered the U.S. position to be more similar to that of "an agitated, blushing debutante. But the young lady is not sensitive. And she wishes you to converse as freely as possible about her, in connection with the UN site—not only about her, but about all the other ladies in the block."

*December 1945*

# BON MOTS

In a speech at the University of Wisconsin, Stevenson had this to say about all the talk that he was an "egghead":

"For a few minutes I took this 'egghead' talk personally in injured silence," he said.

"So far as I could see, it was certainly indisputable that an egghead had given these speeches. But I couldn't stand it and summoned up the courage to ask them what an egghead was.

"The answer, I discovered, is that an egghead is anyone who has gone to college. So at least today I have a lot of company."

Accepting an honorary degree from Dr. Benjamin Wright, President of Smith College, Stevenson remarked:

"How wonderful it must be—to be both Wright and President."

In a speech at Bloomington, Illinois, Stevenson said:

"There has been a lot of flattering talk on the theme of 'home town boy makes good.' It ought to be the other way around—good home town makes boy."

Shortly after the 1962 Cuban missile crisis, Adlai Stevenson introduced President Kennedy at a banquet as:

"Author, producer, and star of Mr. Khrushchev's new play, *A Funny Thing Happened to Me on My Way to Cuba.*"

In 1961, when President Kennedy kept selecting young lawyers such as Newton Minow from Stevenson's Chicago law firm to serve in his Administration, Mr. Stevenson quipped:

"I regret that I have but one law firm to give to my country."

In 1962, Mr. Stevenson discussed the nation's press at a dinner of the Joseph P. Kennedy Foundation:

"I would like to quote a famous newspaper publisher, Joseph Pulitzer, who said, 'Accuracy is to a newspaper what virtue is to a lady.' But I would like to point out that a newspaper can always print a retraction."

When presented with a snowball in 1960 to show how the drive to nominate him for the third time was snowballing, Stevenson quipped:

"Little did I know I had been on ice so long."

Some people had difficulty pronouncing Adlai Stevenson's first name, causing him to comment:

"The correct pronunciation is 'Ad-lay.' Although to put it mildly, I have been called many things."

"The relationship of the toastmaster to the speaker should be the same as that of the fan to the fan dancer. It should call attention to the subject without making any particular effort to cover it."

Shortly after his defeat in the presidential election of 1952, Mr. Stevenson was asked by a reporter in Atlanta, Georgia, "Do you believe the Southerners who voted Republican in 1952 will return to the Democratic party in 1956?"

"Certainly," said Mr. Stevenson, "I believe in the redemption of sin."

"When I was a boy, I was told that anyone could be President, and I believed it."

"Being late with speeches has always been my trouble and twice it cost me the Presidency."

"Any similarity between the party of Lincoln and Joe McCarthy is purely coincidental."

Adlai Stevenson was often criticized for injecting humor into his 1952 campaign speeches. He had two comments on the subject:

"A merry heart is like a medicine but a broken spirit drieth up the bones."

"I refuse to conform to the Republican law of gravity."

Replying to a heckler:
"I believe in the forgiveness of sin and the redemption of ignorance."

*Dallas, Texas*
*October 1963*

"It reminds me of the small boy who jumbled his biblical quotations and said: 'A lie is an abomination unto the Lord, and a very present help in trouble.'"

*Springfield, Illinois*
*January 1951*

"Confronted, surrounded indeed, as I am here in Cambridge tonight by more highly educated fellow citizens than I have ever faced, and inadequately prepared, I am uncomfortably reminded of the abiding truth of those classic words that never occurred to Horace: '*Via ovicipitum dura est,*' or for the benefit of the engineers among you: 'The way of the egghead is hard.'"

*Harvard University Lecture*
*March 1954*

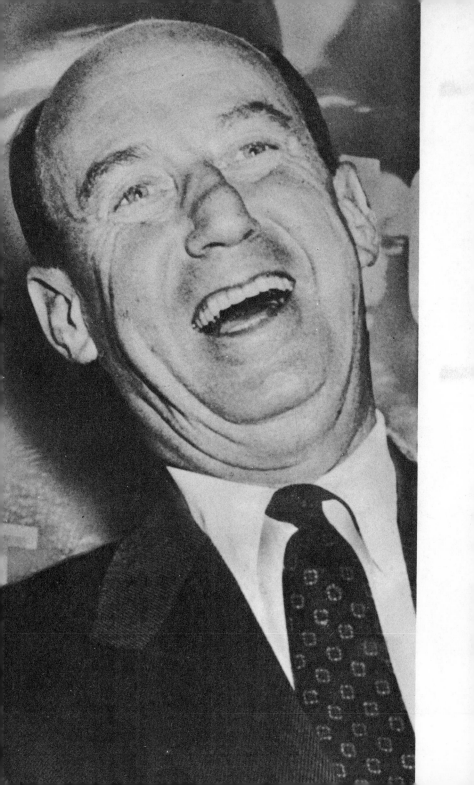

"An editor is one who separates the wheat from the chaff and prints the chaff."

Stevenson once greeted a friend selected for an important position:

"Congratulations on your election as president. I know from hearsay how satisfying that can be."

Stevenson on taxes:

"There was a time when a fool and his money were soon parted, but now it happens to everybody."

To his critics, who accused him during the 1952 presidential campaign of being "an egghead," he commented:

"Eggheads unite—you have nothing to lose but your yolks."


"When I was a boy, I never had much sympathy for a holiday speaker. He was just kind of an interruption between the hot dogs and a fly in the lemonade."

*Flint, Michigan*
1952

"I sometimes marvel at the extraordinary docility with which Americans submit to speeches."

*Chicago, Illinois*
*1950*

"I live in a woman's club. For a number of years, the Woman's Club and Amateur Music Club have held meetings on the first floor of the Executive Mansion. Now you can imagine my feelings when I forget a meeting is on and pop in unannounced."

*Springfield, Illinois*

"I have been in the doghouse more than once and cannot say that I minded. I have always enjoyed the company of dogs. As a child I found comfort in the doghouse. After childish misdeeds followed by reprimands I would retire there. On one occasion I fell asleep and my concerned parents found me only after exhausting all other possibilities.

My parents were vitamin-conscious. How often my mother used to call me at play from the door, 'Adlai, come and get your orange juice,' a call that did not make me popular with new playmates! I rarely take orange juice now."

*Springfield, Illinois*

"People make up their minds about who's right or wrong with little or no knowledge of the facts. Most of them react like the tired mother when she hears bickering in the backyard. 'Go see what Willie's doing and tell him not to.'"

*Flint, Michigan*
*April 1952*

"The lowest of jewelry thieves is the robber of that precious jewel of another's time."

*Springfield, Illinois*

"If laughter is an intoxicant, I am perpetually tight."

Adlai E. Stevenson was awarded the Distinguished Civilian Service Award in 1945. The morning after the event the Washington *Post* illustrated its story of the award with a photograph of the first Adlai E. Stevenson in his last years. Stevenson clipped the story and mailed it with a note to his friend Wayne Coy of the *Post's* editorial staff.

"Ho hum," he wrote, "I've a white mustache and a wing collar and I'm seventy, and all the time I thought I was a young man in the very mold of fashion. But then perhaps it's just as well we see ourselves as others see us and the resemblance would be very surprising to grandfather, dead these thirty-five years."

As a presidential candidate in 1952, Stevenson was America's number one bachelor. Rumors about mythical romances ran hot and heavy. Every week new fiancées were linked with Stevenson, causing the presidential candidate to comment:

"They must think the plural of spouse is spice."

"I'm like the everlasting optimist who fell off a skyscraper. As he passed the twentieth floor, the horrified spectators in windows heard him shout, 'So far, so good!'"

1950

At a dinner in New York sponsored by the Friars Club, Master of Ceremonies George Jessel called on Stevenson to speak after the guests had roared at some remarks by Fred Allen. Stevenson was unprepared and did the only thing he could think of. He said:

"Ladies and gentlemen, during the course of the dinner, Mr. Allen and I were discussing what we would say here

tonight. We traded manuscripts so that each of us could take a look at the other's speech. You have just heard Mr. Allen deliver my speech. And I must say he delivered it very well. As for Mr. Allen's speech, I have it here but I don't think it would amuse you."

"I am a great believer in national humility, modesty, self-examination, and self-criticism, and I have preached these virtues vigorously, although, of course, I haven't practiced them very diligently."

*Columbia University*
*June 5, 1954*

"I have sometimes said that flattery is all right—if you don't inhale."

*February 1, 1961*

"I have never believed that whiskers and wisdom are necessarily synonymous; sometimes, indeed, whiskers merely adorn blank spaces on blank faces."

In a speech at Radcliffe College:
"Do you know the difference between a beautiful woman and a charming one? A beauty is a woman you notice, a charmer is one who notices you."

*1963*

"Man does not live by words alone, despite the fact that sometimes he has to eat them."

*1952 Campaign*